SQUIRE

WORKBOOK 1

TEENS

SQUIRE

VALOR - TEENS

Printed by IngramSpark

ISBN: 979-8-218-54760-8

Welcome to the "Valor" series!

ACKNOWLEDGEMENTS

The Valor™ series, including its booklets and workbooks, has been the product of ongoing clinical and coaching work with teens and college-aged young men since 2007. I am grateful for the courage of these young men as they worked through personal challenges. They've provided immense insight into various clinical issues. I also cannot ignore the insights of adults in various sex addiction treatment programs who requested the Valor group – wishing they'd had something similar when they were younger.

SQUIRE

WORKBOOK 1

TEENS

Contents

INTRODUCTION TO ATTRIBUTES

Welcome to the VALOR program—a place where young men like you take the first steps toward reclaiming your strength and purpose. This journey is about becoming the best version of yourself, and we're here to equip you with the tools, guidance, and encouragement you need. To overcome problems with pornography or sexually compulsive behaviors isn't easy—it requires focus, discipline, and effort—but with persistence and dedication, success is inevitable!

In the VALOR series, you'll have the opportunity to earn "ranks" that represent your progress and growth. Each rank builds on the lessons you've learned and tasks you've completed, helping you become stronger and confident with every step forward.

You've got what it takes to succeed. Stay committed, and remember—you're not alone on the journey!

Ranks

Page

A medieval page demonstrated a willingness to learn, and prepared himself for the role of a squire by mastering essential skills, listening to his mentors, and embracing the discipline required for knighthood. This rank represents the start of your journey. You recognize that you need help and ask for support. You set aside your pride, complete the initial tasks, and commit to the process.

Squire

The medieval squire advanced from his role as a page to take on greater responsibilities, proving his readiness through dedicated learning, skillful training, and significant progress in his journey toward knighthood. In this rank you learn key concepts and complete tasks that promote your growth. You will learn more about the nature of addiction, the importance of boundaries, recognizing triggers, and addressing toxic shame. Additionally, you learn how your brain works.

Archer

The medieval archer progressed from his role as a squire to master greater precision, honing his skills through disciplined practice and demonstrating remarkable improvement in his craft. This rank builds on the self-awareness you're developing, and moves you forward with greater precision. You will understand yourself deeper and learn about styles of acting out, challenges of growing up, the importance of connection, and how to use tools to interrupt and stop compulsive behavior. This rank emphasizes acting with intention and foresight.

Sergeant

The medieval sergeant advanced from his position as an archer, having proven his knowledge and capability, ready to take on greater responsibilities as he continued to progress and learn. This rank builds on the focus you've developed, and moves into greater responsibility. You learn about the impact of the digital world on your behavior, the importance of building a support team, and the value of grit. You will explore emotional issues that get sexualized, and gain deeper insights into your own responses. This rank emphasizes teamwork, structure, accountability, and strengthening your ability to inspire others.

Captain

The medieval captain rose from his position as a sergeant, having further demonstrated his ability, grown in strength and skill, and shown he was ready to guide and support others in their development. This rank moves you into leadership, where stronger sobriety and service to others in the group is an expectation. At this rank, you learn more about friendships, changes in your body, emotional energy, and what healthy sexuality looks like. This rank expects you to be a role model of integrity and support, using your personal growth to guide and encourage others.

Knight

The medieval knight excelled as a captain, continuously growing in strength and skill while helping others, ultimately earning the great honor of knighthood as a shining example of dedication and leadership. This rank represents the culmination of all the lessons and skills developed in the previous ranks. You are expected to have a stronger sobriety from compulsive behaviors and to demonstrate transparency, authenticity, and a willingness to support others in the group. You will learn about healthy affection, and review memories and negative messages you may have internalized. You will also dive into the story of Cole Matthews from Touching Spirit Bear to gain insights into his recovery. As part of this final rank, you will complete a self-assessment to evaluate your progress toward lasting recovery, ensuring you are prepared to continue on the journey with courage.

Stay strong and remember that **persistence** is your greatest ally. Changes may be difficult at times, but don't give up—you're stronger than you realize. This journey is a marathon not a sprint, so be patient with yourself. Focus on the big picture, celebrate each small victory, and trust that you're on the path to lasting freedom and success. You have what it takes to overcome this! Keep moving forward with courage and determination. Welcome to Valor—this is your place to rise and thrive!

Congratulations on joining a Valor group! It takes a lot of courage to recognize that you need help, and committing to this program shows your dedication to making a positive change in your life. Your first step is to complete the items below for your status as a "Page." This initiates you into the group.

PAGE

1. Talk to someone you trust about your struggle with pornography or other sexual problems. Be honest and explain why you need help.
2. Receive "The Armory" booklet and start reading it.
3. Agree to keep all the Valor group discussions and names private; this means you will not share with anyone the specific stories or names of people in your group.

Date Completed: _______________________________

Once completed, you'll be starting this journey at the rank of "**Page**," and working toward the rank of "Squire." This is the first rank in the series, and it's the foundation for improvement. You'll work through specific tasks and lessons that will help you understand basic concepts and build a solid support network. The tasks will challenge you, but will also empower you with tools and knowledge you need to succeed.

Once you've completed all the required tasks and lessons in the Squire workbook, you'll be awarded the rank of Squire. This is a big achievement and a testament to your hard work and commitment. Remember, every step you take brings you closer to overcoming your challenges and becoming the person you want to be.

Good luck, and remember, you're not alone on this journey. We're all here to support each other.

SQUIRE

TASKS

1. Confirm completion of the tasks for rank of PAGE.
   Date: _________________ Initial: _________________

2. Read the first portion of The Armory and discuss with your counselor or coach.
   Date: _________________ Initial: _________________

3. Share your story with your Valor group, and talk about any hiding and shame.
   Date: _________________ Initial: _________________

4. Contact a member of your Valor group outside of group time, and share a list of all the positive things you like about yourself. Report to the group what this was like for you.
   Date: _________________ Initial: _________________

5. Complete Lesson One and discuss with your counselor or coach.
   Date: _________________ Initial: _________________

6. Complete Lesson Two and discuss with your counselor or coach.
   Date: _________________ Initial: _________________

7. Complete Lesson Three and discuss with your counselor or coach.
   Date: _________________ Initial: _________________

8. Complete Lesson Four and discuss with your counselor or coach.

   Date: _________________ Initial: _________________

LESSON ONE

Habit or Compulsion or Addiction?

SQUIRE

WORKBOOK 1

LESSON ONE

Habit or Compulsion or Addiction?

Is your problem with pornography (or other sexual behavior) simply a habit, does it feel compulsive, or has it escalated into addiction? Knowing the difference is important.

Habit - Compulsion - Addiction

A habit is something you do regularly, often without thinking about it. It's a behavior that has become automatic. As an illustration, brushing your teeth every morning is a habit, and you do it without much thought because it's part of your daily routine.

A compulsion is when you can't stop yourself and feel out of control. At certain times, the urges become intense and you find yourself doing things you didn't want to do. It's like your brain got hijacked. Using the previous illustration, brushing your teeth feels like something you need to do multiple times a day even when it's unnecessary; it's hard to stop yourself.

Addiction on the other hand, is a behavior that gets compulsive, but feels as though you _need_ it to feel normal. Things don't feel right without it. Addiction slowly takes over your life, affecting the way you think, the way you feel, your daily activities, relationships, and overall well-being. Once again using our illustration, brushing your teeth feels like something you need to do multiple times a day and it's hard to stop yourself even when it interferes with other things, or you simply don't feel "okay" until after you've done it.

Talk to your counselor or coach about your own situation. Sometimes, what starts as simple curiosity can spiral into something more serious. Many teens are struggling with pornography or sexual behavior because it's a habit or a compulsion, but not necessarily because they are addicted. To keep things in the workbook simple we are going to use the word addiction to describe the problem when it's out of control. But remember… this doesn't necessarily mean you are addicted.

Here's some questions to consider:

Need for More

You might notice the need for more screen time to get the same 'high,' which indicates that your brain is asking for more to achieve the same effect. Over time, you may start using pornography more often and for longer periods. If you find it hard to stop and feel like you're losing self-control, this could be a sign of addiction.

Have you been increasing the amount of time you spend watching porn or doing sexual things?

❏ YES ❏ NO

Do you feel like you need to watch or do more to get the same 'high'?

❏ YES ❏ NO

Are you finding it hard to stop; feeling like you've lost self-control?

❏ YES ❏ NO

Life Takes a Hit

If your grades, job, relationships, sports activities, or friend groups are suffering because you're too caught up watching porn, it's a serious issue. Spending time on porn or sexual activity, when you should be focused on other important things might indicate that you're developing an addiction.

Have you missed activities or responsibilities because of porn or sexual activity?

❑ YES ❑ NO

Has porn or sexual activities affected your relationships with family or friends?

❑ YES ❑ NO

Have your friends commented that you seem less involved or distant from them?

❑ YES ❑ NO

Are you struggling more socialling now than you used to? Perhaps you have a more difficult time picking up social cues, interacting with people, or responding to others?

❑ YES ❑ NO

Negative Vibes

Watching pornography can make some teenage boys feel bad about themselves. It can wear down your confidence and self-esteem. Sometimes, you might even hate yourself afterwards.

Do you feel bad about yourself after watching porn or doing sexual things?

❑ YES ❑ NO

Has your confidence dropped since you started watching porn or doing sexual things?

❑ YES ❑ NO

Do you ever get mad at yourself after watching porn or doing sexual things?

❑ YES ❑ NO

Do you find yourself more "reactive" or impulsive when making decisions?

❑ YES ❑ NO

Can't Quit

If you've tried to cut down or stop using porn (or doing sexual things) but just couldn't, that's a possible sign of a developing addiction. Feeling like you need it is another strong indicator that you might be dealing with addiction.

Have you made efforts to quit or reduce watching porn or doing sexual things, but then returned to it again?

❑ YES ❑ NO

Do you ever feel powerless to control the sexual urges?

❑ YES ❑ NO

Does it ever seem like you need porn or sexual activity in order to feel okay?

❑ YES ❑ NO

Mood Swings

Turning to pornography or sexual activity when you're feeling depressed, anxious, bored, lonely, stressed, or just low is another possible danger sign. If you feel like you need porn or sexual things to cope with emotion, it's possible that you might be developing an addiction.

Do you ever use porn or sexual activity as a way to relax from stress?

❑ YES ❑ NO

Do you get irritable or moody when you can't use porn or do something sexual?

❑ YES ❑ NO

Do you use porn or sexual activities when you get depressed, sad, anxious, bored, lonely, frustrated or angry?

❑ YES ❑ NO

Do you have a difficult time feeling or expressing emotions?

❑ YES ❑ NO

Are there times you are uncertain what you are feeling?

❑ YES ❑ NO

Do you have a hard time understanding what someone else is feeling?

❑ YES ❑ NO

Do you ever feel "numb" or empty from any emotion?

❑ YES ❑ NO

Values or Morals

You might find that watching porn or doing certain sexual things conflicts with your personal values or morals. You might even promise others or God that you'll stop, but then keep going back to it.

Does watching porn or doing certain sexual things ever conflict with your personal values or standards?

❑ YES ❑ NO

Have you made promises to yourself, to God, or to others that you'll stop but then return to it again?

❑ YES ❑ NO

Withdrawal

When people get addicted to sex or pornography, and then try to stop, they might experience withdrawal symptoms. These can include difficulty sleeping, restlessness, irritability, body aches, headaches, moodiness, depression, anxiety, aching testicles or other sensations in the mind and body.

When you try to stop, have you experienced any physical symptoms like problems with restlessness, headaches, or body aches?

❑ YES ❑ NO

When you try to stop, have you experienced any emotional symptoms like irritability, moodiness, depression or anxiety?

❏ YES ❏ NO

Have you made promises to yourself, to God, or to others that you'll stop but then return to it again?

❏ YES ❏ NO

When you try to stop, do you get obsessed with sexual thoughts throughout the day?

❏ YES ❏ NO

When you try to stop, do you have difficulty sleeping at night?

❏ YES ❏ NO

When you try to stop, do you feel more anxious or depressed?

❏ YES ❏ NO

Reflection and Honesty

If any of the above applies to you, you might be headed toward addiction. It's crucial to be honest with yourself about this. When habits become compulsive or addictive, they can slowly destroy your life. The danger is that addiction usually escalates and gets worse over time.

1. In the space provided, write down whether you think your issue is a habit, a compulsion or an addiction. Include your reasons:

____

____

____

____

____

2. Have you experienced any of the withdrawal symptoms listed previously? Write these here and discuss them with your counselor or coach.

____

____

____

____

____

Sobriety & Recovery

Sobriety means you're not acting out sexually. When someone asks if you're sober, they're asking if you've done anything sexually you promised to stop. You're NOT "sober" if you've slipped into a sexual behavior you're trying to stop. Staying sober is about managing your body's impulses to act out sexually.

Recovery on the other hand, is about changing yourself on the inside, so that sobriety happens naturally. When you handle your emotions and needs in healthy ways, the bad habits naturally fade away. Recovery is about reshaping your life from the inside. If you're working with a counselor or coach, they will guide you.

Keep in mind, staying sober is not the same as recovery. You could stop all sexual activity and still not be in recovery. Your goal in this program will be to develop a recovery lifestyle so that sobriety is easier for you to achieve.

3. Sobriety means you're not ____ .

4. Recovery is about changing yourself on the _______________________, so that sobriety is easier for you to achieve.

Authenticity & Transparency

Admitting that you have a problem with pornography or sexual behavior requires honesty with yourself. This might be the first time you've accepted that the problem is out of control and you need help. Maybe you've been hiding for a long time and avoiding the truth. Being real with yourself is called being **authentic**, and is necessary to get better. When you decide to openly share with others, we call it being **transparent**, which is also necessary for recovery.

Some people wear different masks to keep others from seeing them. These masks show one thing on the outside while hiding what's on the inside. For example, somebody might act like the class-clown, but deep down they're really insecure. Maybe another guy acts like he's perfect and doesn't have problems, when he's really struggling with serious challenges.

5. What are some of the masks people might wear to hide their feelings or struggles?

____

____

____

____

____

____

____

Masks help people portray a certain image, while hiding their feelings or insecurities. It prevents someone from opening up. Others can't see what's really going on behind the mask. People wear masks for different reasons, but ultimately they are trying to protect themselves.

6. Read the list below and mark any items that you think would cause a person to wear a "mask":

❑ Embarrassment   ❑ Disgust

❑ Punishment   ❑ Will get rejected

❑ Disappointment   ❑ Will get teased

❑ Criticism   ❑ Won't fit in

❑ Shame   ❑ Will become a burden

❑ Guilt   ❑ Other: _______________________

❑ Fear

7. Write down the different masks that YOU wear to protect yourself:

____

____

____

____

____

____

8. What are your masks protecting you from?

____

____

____

____

____

Living without a mask means being real (authentic) with yourself and others, and that can bring discomfort. Guys usually wear masks to avoid the costs of being "seen." When you decide to take off your mask and be authentic, you might face emotions like fear, vulnerability, criticism, guilt, shame or rejection. The costs of being "seen" could include losing friends who don't accept you or dealing with criticism from others. However, being authentic is worth it in the long run and builds a recovery lifestyle. The gains from living authentically are usually much better and less painful in the long-run. To be "seen" has more beneficial gains than costs.

9. What might be the costs and the gains from taking off your mask and being authentic? Think about your own situation and fill in the boxes:

COSTS	GAINS
Example: My dad might get really disappointed and start giving me a lecture.	*Example: Things will finally be in the open and I'll have my parents help. No more secrets.*

Denial

Denial is when you refuse to acknowledge something because it's too difficult or painful to accept. It's like convincing yourself that everything is fine even when it's not. This can prevent you from dealing with problems and getting help.

Escaping denial means facing the truth about yourself. This causes you to become more authentic. When you stop pretending and start being real, you confront what you've been avoiding. The more you practice, the better you'll get, and the easier it will become to handle difficult feelings or situations. Over time, being honest with yourself will become more normal and lead to a healthier life.

10. Have you been in denial and avoiding your problems? Describe in the space provided:

____

____

____

____

____

____

____

11. In an effort to escape denial, take some time to consider your own story. When your problems first began, what types of feelings or emotions did you have? Circle all that apply.

Confused	Relieved	Curious
Angry	Shame	Depressed
Aroused	Anxious	Embarrassed
Alone	Excited	Worried
Fear	Sad	Stressed Out
Hopeful	Nervous	Happy
Frustrated	Dead	Other _______________
Guilty	Sinful	Other _______________
Scared	Grateful	

12. Write down the story of when your problem first started and what happened.

____

____

____

____

____

____

____

13. Describe what finally happened that caused you to ask for help? Did anyone get involved?

____

____

____

____

____

____

14. Now that you've started getting support, what emotions do you have? Circle all that apply.

Confused	Relieved	Curious
Angry	Shame	Depressed
Aroused	Anxious	Embarrassed
Alone	Excited	Worried
Fear	Sad	Stressed Out
Hopeful	Nervous	Happy
Frustrated	Dead	Other _____________
Guilty	Sinful	Other _____________
Scared	Grateful	

Congratulations on completing this lesson. You are no longer hiding or pretending. You are becoming more *authentic* and *transparent*. This is the road to healthy living!

NOTES

____

____

____

____

____

____

____

____

____

____

____

____

LESSON TWO

Boundaries & Bottom Lines

SQUIRE

WORKBOOK 1

LESSON TWO

Boundaries

Boundaries are key to keeping relationships healthy and staying true to yourself. There are two types: internal and external. Internal boundaries are the rules you set for yourself—like deciding not to scroll on social media all night so you can get enough sleep. It's about saying no to yourself and keeping control of your thoughts and actions. External boundaries are about how you interact with others, like asking a friend to give you personal space, letting them know your time is important, or standing firm when someone tries to pressure you into doing something you're not okay with.

Boundaries also play a big role in friendships and dating. They can involve things like how much affection or time you're comfortable sharing, or setting clear limits to make sure others respect you. It might also include catching your thoughts and behaviors, and telling yourself "no" even though you want to do something. Patrick Carnes once stated, "Part of being grown up is making your body do what it does not want to do," (Carnes, 2015, p. 169). When you stick to your boundaries, it shows that you value yourself and others.

If you're working to overcome compulsive sexual behaviors, setting clear boundaries is essential. A good place to start is with external boundaries—specifically by establishing your "bottom lines," the clear limits you don't allow yourself or others to cross.

Bottom Lines & Triggers

Bottom Lines

Bottom lines are the behaviors you're trying to stop. When you set your bottom lines, you're making a promise with yourself not to cross that line. Setting bottom lines gives you a clear boundary toward your goal. By creating your own bottom lines, you can stay focused and committed.

Take Kyle for instance who created the following bottom lines:

> 1. I will not masturbate.
> 2. I will not look at pornography.
> 3. I will not have sex with my girlfriend.

After you set your bottom lines, it's crucial to share them with someone you trust. Let them know these are the behaviors you're working to stop. Being clear about your bottom lines and talking to someone about them will give you more support and courage.

1. Take a few moments to decide on your bottom lines and write them in the space provided:

____

____

____

____

____

____

____

____

____

____

Addressing issues under the surface is crucial in this process but takes time. You need to stay consistent in making changes if you want to shift your thoughts and feelings. Long-term success requires long-term commitment. Remember, this is a marathon, not a sprint.

Personal Rules

Now that you've established bottom lines, your next step is to create personal rules. Rules help you stick to your boundaries and avoid "slips." A slip would be doing something sexual that you're trying to stop. Personal rules aren't just about avoiding problems; they're about staying safely away from potential slips. Think of them as a safety net that keeps you out of risky situations that could pull you back into old habits. For example, if your goal is to avoid watching porn, a personal rule could be not using your phone or computer alone at night. These rules help you stay strong and make it easier to avoid slipping up.

Here's Matthew's Personal Rules:

1. Take short five-minute showers.
2. Only use my laptop when someone else is around.
3. Ask my dad to check my phone history every night.
4. Keep my phone out of my room at bedtime.
5. Never take my girlfriend into my bedroom.

Notice how each of Matthew's personal rules simply try to keep him away from problems. They don't stop sexual urges, they just give him extra buffer from difficult situations.

2. Think about some personal rules that would help YOU to keep your bottom lines. Write them down here:

1. ____

2. ____

3. ____

4. ____

5. ____

Triggers

Triggers are like a loaded gun, ready to go off when the trigger is pulled. When you encounter a trigger, it can quickly set off thoughts and behaviors that make it hard to stay in control. Recognizing your triggers helps you avoid them, keeping you on track. By knowing what sets you off, you can plan ahead and use tools to steer clear of those situations.

Understanding your triggers is key to taking back control. It's about being prepared before those urges hit. There are three main types of triggers you should be aware of. Discuss them with your counselor or coach to see how they relate to you. Remember, triggers aren't bad—they just push your mind toward sexual thoughts and actions. By recognizing and managing them, you can stay on course and make positive changes.

The following are a list of the three categories of triggers:

SENSORY: these triggers are things you see, hear, taste, touch, or smell. For example:

- *The smell of perfume in math class triggers Keyton.*
- *Trevor gets triggered walking down the hall when girls accidentally brush his arm.*
- *William gets triggered when a notification pops up on his phone.*

EMOTIONAL: these are feelings like sadness, anger, fear, happy, embarrassed, depressed, frustrated, rejected, alone, stressed, overwhelmed, or just plain bored. For example:

- *Zach gets angry when he argues with his mom and stomps off to his room.*
- *Tyler sinks into depression when he gets rejected by his friend group.*
- *Kyle gets unsettled when someone unfriends him on social media.*

SITUATIONAL: these are specific places, times, or scenarios. For example:

- *Brandon gets triggered during Christmas break when there's no schedule.*
- *Zane finds it tough when he's home alone and the house is empty.*
- *Kellen gets irritated whenever someone comments rudely on one of his posts.*

Don't fear your triggers. Instead, learn to respond with intention. When you understand your triggers and how they push you toward your limits, you'll feel more confident in handling them.

3. What are some "sensory" triggers for you?

\

\

\

\

\

4. What are some "emotional" triggers for you?

\

\

\

\

\

\

\

5. What are some "situation" triggers for you?

\

\

\

\

\

\

\

6. Can you think of any additional triggers that don't fit the previous categories?

____

____

____

____

____

____

Plan Ahead for Triggers

Take some time to think about what you do during the day and week to help identify when your triggers usually occur. If you know when you're more at risk, you can plan ahead and avoid problems. By being prepared, you won't be caught off guard by sexual urges, and you'll feel more in control and able to stay on track.

What are some things you do every day? Where do you usually go? What do you do at school? Where do you hang out after school? Do you have a church group or a club you attend? What about weekends—do you have any special plans with friends on the weekend? Are there family activities or group events coming up? Are there days or times you specifically get stressed, tired, bored, lonely or anxious? Knowing your routine can help you spot and manage your triggers better.

7. Consider your weekly routine and the questions above, write down triggers that could happen this week:

____

____

____

____

____

____

8. Now, think about a plan for these triggers. What can you do to avoid or reduce them before they happen? For example:

- **Jonathon:** _I usually get really triggered and slip with porn on Sunday night because I'm dreading going back to school. I can stay up with my mom and help her with cleanup, then keep my bedroom door open at bedtime._

- **Tyler:** *Next Friday is tryouts for basketball and I'm really anxious. I'm not as good as some of the other guys. I'm scared of looking stupid or embarrassing myself. I can call my best friend and ask for some encouragement.*

NOTES

LESSON THREE

Releasing Toxic Shame

SQUIRE

WORKBOOK 1

LESSON THREE

Releasing Toxic Shame

A big part of getting better is learning to feel good about yourself despite any problems or mistakes you've made. It's important to value who you are. When you have healthy self-esteem, it becomes easier to express your thoughts and feelings openly. This is what we call living authentically. We've discussed this before, but let's review it.

Think about this: if someone wants to see a genuine Picasso painting, they go to the Louvre museum in France to see the real thing, not a copy. The same goes for wanting an authentic pair of Nike shoes—you'd go to a store that sells the original, not a knock-off. Living authentically is similar. It means being real and true about your thoughts, feelings, and emotions.

Sometimes, you'll notice that both adults and teenagers pretend to be something they're not to hide their feelings or thoughts. People often do this to protect themselves from embarrassment or shame. It's like in a video game when you put on different "skins" to change how your character looks. You can adjust things like armor, colors, or other features to create a specific image. This is similar to building an "avatar" that shows the traits you want others to see.

People often wear "masks" or create "avatars" to present a different image that hides how they feel. They might be ashamed of who they are or what they've done, so they put on a mask to cover their emotions. When someone struggles with self-acceptance, using a mask can seem like a way to protect themselves from rejection or judgment. Recovery means letting go of that shame and allowing others to see the real you. Have you noticed others wearing masks to hide? Write down any examples you can think of.

Example: *Jonathan is always laughing and joking, acting like a class-clown, even though he's depressed and anxious.*

Example: *Brian brings his Bible to church every Sunday and acts like he never has any problems, even though he's secretly struggling with vape and doesn't want anyone to know.*

1. ____

____

____

____

____

____

____

____

Guilt vs. Shame

Understanding the difference between guilt and shame is important. Feeling guilty about a mistake or something you did wrong is normal—everyone experiences it from time to time. Guilt can be healthy because it helps you reflect on your actions and encourages you to make better choices in the future.

Toxic shame is like a poison that takes guilt to an extreme level. Instead of just feeling bad about a mistake, it turns against you, attacking your sense of self-worth. Over time, it eats away at your confidence, much like a cancer. Take a look at the chart and see if you can tell the difference:

GUILT	TOXIC SHAME
I feel bad…	I am bad…
I made a mistake…	I am a mistake…
It was wrong…	Something is wrong with me…
I failed…	I am a failure…
My effort wasn't good enough…	I am not good enough…

2. In your own words, describe the difference between guilt and toxic shame:

____

____

____

____

____

____

____

____

____

____

It's crucial to understand that toxic shame fuels all compulsive and addictive behaviors. Whether you're dealing with drugs, alcohol, gambling, or pornography, toxic shame will always make the problem worse. The more intense the shame, the stronger the addiction. To lessen the intensity of your struggle, start working on removing the toxic shame within you. Some guys even notice that they act out more when their shame is high.

3. What types of "shame" messages do you hear about yourself? Maybe talk to someone you trust and ask them what they think. Use the previous chart to brainstorm ideas.

Example: *When I saw porn the first time I immediately felt shocked, then started to hate myself because I kind of liked it. It was gross… how could I like that stuff? I must be a disgusting person!*

____

____

____

____

____

____

____

Toxic shame fills your mind with negative thoughts about yourself, making you want to give up. Have you ever felt so low that you just wanted to give up on life? Those feelings come from toxic shame. It doesn't feel good and can drag you down even further.

Guilt, on the other hand, points out your mistakes but motivates you to try harder. It pushes you to improve yourself and set goals. Although uncomfortable, guilt inspires you to become a better person.

Four Core Beliefs

Mental health professionals have identified four common beliefs among those who struggle with compulsive pornography or sexual behavior. These beliefs might develop during childhood or after the problem begins, and they are deeply unhealthy. They stem from toxic shame and, in turn, feed into it, creating a harmful cycle.

Toxic Core Beliefs

- *I'm not good enough – I'm bad/unworthy.*

- *I can't trust or depend on others to help me with my needs.*

- *If anyone really knew me for who I am, they would not love me.*

- *Sexual feelings have taken over my life – I can't live without them.*

4. Which of these four core beliefs do you relate to the most?

____

____

____

____

____

5. Describe a recent time when one of these core beliefs showed up in your life.

____

____

____

____

6. When these toxic beliefs pop into your mind, have you noticed how they make you feel? Take a moment to write down any feelings they cause. For example, *"When my friends leave me out, I start to feel like no one could ever like me for who I am. I feel rejected and depressed, and sometimes it even makes my stomach hurt."*

____

____

____

____

7. How do you think these core beliefs might affect your confidence?

____

____

____

____

____

Isolation Trap

When your mind is filled with toxic core beliefs, it opens the door to toxic shame. This shame often leads to isolation, where people start hiding their thoughts and feelings. Even if someone has a large group of friends, toxic shame can cause them to shut down emotionally and stop sharing. They begin to hide parts of themselves behind a mask, feeling so ashamed and embarrassed that they pull away from others. Even though they might be physically around people, they shut them out emotionally, creating more shame and loneliness. This isolation fuels the struggle with porn or sex, making the cycle even harder to break. In the end, **isolation is the lifeblood of compulsive sexual behavior**.

8. Complete this sentence: _______________________________ is the lifeblood of compulsive sexual behavior.

9. Think about a time when you started to pull away from others. Write about it here. (**Example:** *There was a time when my mom got really mad at me. She yelled, and I felt like I couldn't do anything right. I went to my room and ignored my friend's texts. I stayed there the whole day without talking to anyone.*")

10. Can you think of ways to reduce your own isolation when it happens? Refer to the Armory if you need some ideas.

Support Network

Think of a support network as your team—people who help you through your recovery journey. Having a strong team is essential for success. These people not only support you but also help you break free from toxic shame by pulling you out of isolation. Opening up and sharing your struggles can be uncomfortable and embarrassing, and it might be scary to risk judgment or criticism. But even though it's tough, there's nothing more healing than being transparent. Facing your fears is a crucial step in the process.

To build a strong support team and stop hiding, talk to people who feel "safe" to you. Ideally, these are adults who can keep things confidential and won't judge you. A great support person is someone who can listen to your most embarrassing thoughts and still stand by you.

However, not everyone is "safe." Some people can be gossipy, critical, or unkind. Others might be judgmental or offer empty advice, often because they don't know how to support you properly.

11. Who are the adults in your life you believe could be safe and supportive? List as many as you can think of:

____

____

____

____

____

12. Supportive adults might not always know how to create safety in the relationship. Take a look at the statements below that other teens have shared. Check any that apply to you:

❑ I need someone who can listen without judging or criticizing.

❑ I need someone who can handle private or embarrassing things without making it awkward.

❑ I want them to understand that it's hard for me to open up; I'm used to keeping this a secret.

❑ I need them to promise not to share my private stuff with others—no gossip.

❑ I want to know they aren't disappointed in me or disgusted by what I share.

❑ I need to feel that they care about me and will check in on me, even if I don't reach out.

❑ I need them to promise not to give up on me, even if I slip up or feel like quitting.

❑ I need someone who can encourage and lift me up when I'm feeling down.

❑ I need them to be patient and realize this has been really hard and embarrassing for me.

❑ I need them to understand that I've felt hopeless, anxious, depressed, or alone.

❑ I need someone who can ask me direct questions, even if they're a little embarrassing.

❑ I want someone who's willing to learn about recovery, so they can talk to me more easily.

❑ Other: ____

LESSON FOUR

How Your Brain Works

SQUIRE

WORKBOOK 1

LESSON FOUR
How Your Brain Works

Front Brain

The front part of your brain is called the Prefrontal Cortex. This area controls your "higher" functions—things that require you to examine or reason. In other words, **anything that requires you to think and analyze happens** in the front area. For example, when you're taking a test, solving problems, planning a road trip, or memorizing a sports or music routine, you're using the front part of your brain.

Another job of the prefrontal cortex is **to hold back and resist doing things you know you shouldn't. This is called impulse control**, and it's really important when you have big goals to reach. Have you ever tried to quit an old habit but just couldn't? That's because impulse control, managed by the prefrontal cortex, is what helps you resist those urges.

Compulsively using pornography can mess up your prefrontal cortex, which is **like the brakes of your brain. When these brakes are worn out, stopping becomes really hard**. When your front brain is impacted, your "brakes" don't work well.

The good news is that the impact on your brain can be repaired. The brain will rewire itself when you change your habits and behavior. You just have to learn and practice.

1. The front-brain does anything that requires you to ______________ and ______________ .

2. Another job of the front part of your brain is to hold back and ______________________
   you know you shouldn't do. This is called ______________________________ .

3. Using pornography compulsively messes up your prefrontal cortex, which is like the
   ______________________ of your brain.

4. When the "brakes" are worn out in your brain, ______________________ becomes really hard.

Back-Brain

Let's talk about the "Back-Brain," also known as the limbic system. It's an important part of your brain, but it works differently from the front part. **Think of the back-brain as an alarm system.** It's always ready to warn you about danger or threats. **It operates on autopilot, so it doesn't really think or analyze things.** It reacts automatically to situations. For example, when you feel scared, your limbic brain takes over, and you either fight, run away, or freeze. It quickly decides what to do without thinking, just reacting to protect you.

You can teach your body to handle emotions in better ways instead of reacting impulsively. If we let our instincts take control, we might end up in trouble. Learning to manage emotions, impulses, and urges is a key part of growing up. It takes practice to control how you respond.

When LeBron James was younger, trash talk used to bother him and make him lose focus. Wanting to be the best, he put in the effort to manage his emotions and stay calm. In the NBA Finals, with the game on the line and everyone watching, he stayed composed and made the game-winning shot. LeBron's ability to stay cool under pressure made him a champion and a legend. Just like LeBron, **you have to learn to handle difficult triggers and urges when they happen.** You can learn to use recovery tools instead of falling into old bad habits.

5. The back-brain is like an __________________ system. It operates on __________________, so it doesn't really think or analyze things.

6. Similar to LeBron James, you have to learn to handle difficult __________________ and __________________ when they happen, instead of slipping.

Take a look at these brain scan images. The first image shows what a normal human brain looks like without any influence from addictive behaviors or substances. The lighter areas indicate healthy brain activity, while the darker areas represent spots in the brain that aren't active.

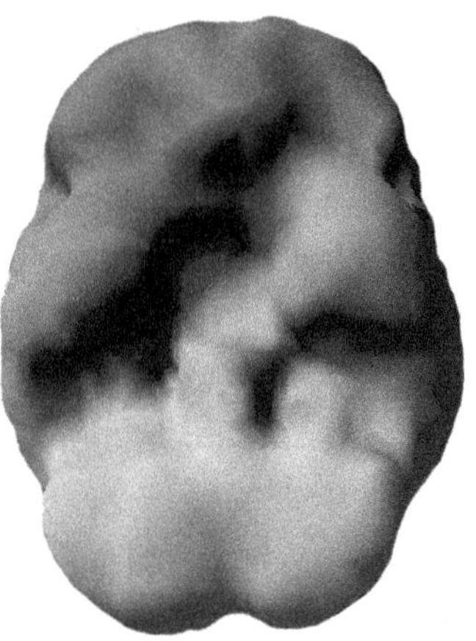

Normal Brain Activity

Now, take a look at the next brain scan image. This shows a human brain affected by compulsive pornography or other sexual behaviors. Notice the darker areas that look like holes. They aren't holes, but actually parts of the front brain that have stopped activity and aren't being used anymore.

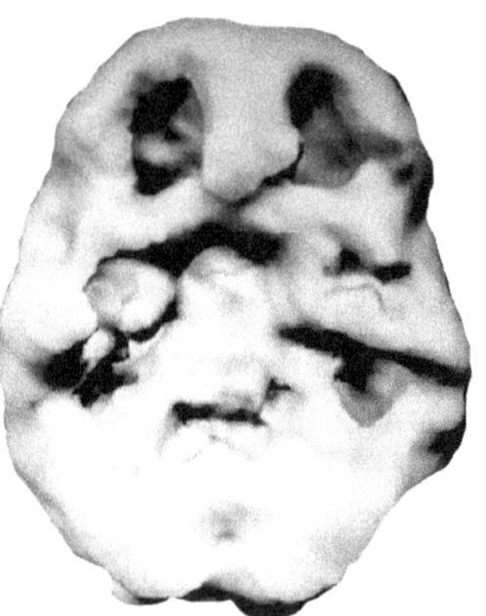

Affected Brain Activity

When the front part of your brain starts to shut down, it causes three specific problems that most people notice when struggling with pornography or sexual addiction:

1. Lack of impulse control.

2. Degrading social abilities.

3. Difficulty processing emotions.

Even if you don't notice these symptoms right away, they gradually appear over time. When someone lacks impulse control, they tend to make quick decisions without fully thinking things through, often leading to poor choices.

When a person's social abilities are affected, they find it more difficult to say the right thing, interact with friends, or pick up on social cues. The person may start to feel more socially awkward or out of place.

When a person has difficulty processing emotions, they might find themselves overwhelmed when emotions arise. It may be tough to know what they are feeling or how to express the emotions.

7. When a person lacks impulse control, they tend to make quick decisions without fully ____________________ things through.

8. When a person's social abilities are affected, they find it more difficult to say the ____________________, interact with ____________________, or pick up on ____________________.

9. When a person has difficulty processing emotions, it may be touch ____________________ what they are feeling, or how to ____________________ the emotions.

The Compulsion Cycle

It's normal to have sexual feelings as a young man. But when those feelings lead to compulsive behaviors, they usually follow a pattern. It begins in your brain when something feels off, either in your body or your surroundings. For instance, you might feel upset, frustrated, or lonely, and that can trigger the cycle. The cycle starts with discomfort. It doesn't have to be extreme pain—just feeling uneasy or uncomfortable can set it off.

When someone feels that distress, it's easy to disconnect and pull away from others, almost like you're retreating into yourself. This isolation leads to obsession over sexual thoughts and behavior. Notice the compulsive cycle chart:

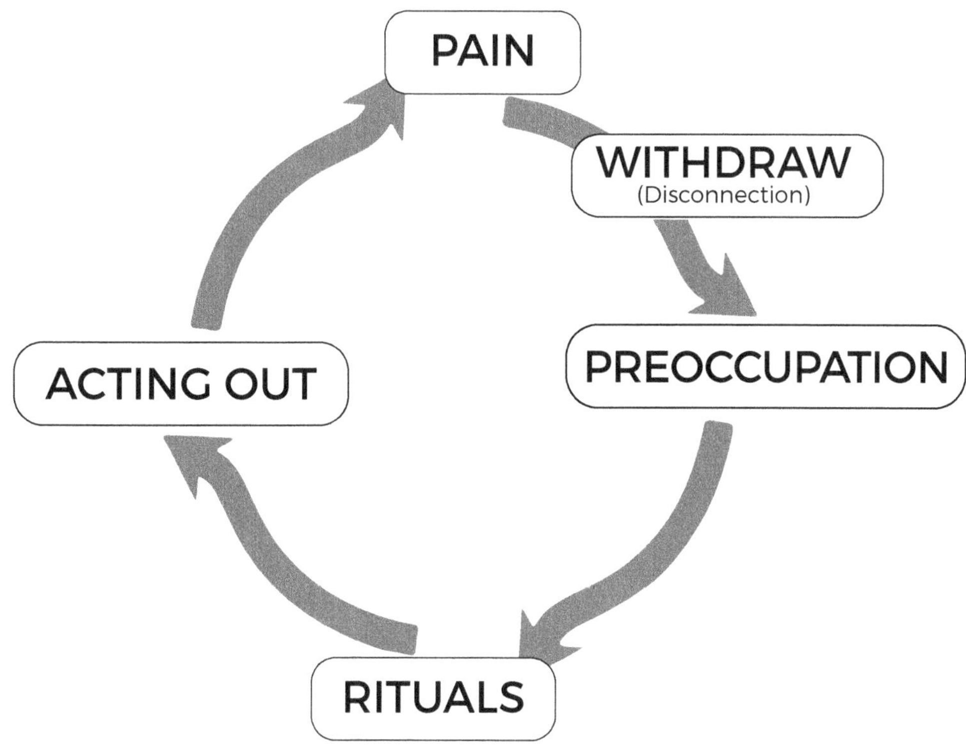

Preoccupation

When you can't shake off sexual thoughts or urges, you're in a preoccupation phase. It feels obsessive, like the images won't leave you alone. You might try to push them away, but if they keep returning, you're stuck in preoccupation. It might feel like you can't control it.

Rituals

When the thoughts and images remain in your head long enough, you will eventually fall into a ritual - this is the behavior that happens right before acting out. These rituals become part of your set-up for acting out. For example, Erik shared his experience: *"Whenever I was really distracted at school, I went home and told my mom I was going to my room to finish homework. I took out my laptop and locked the door. Going to my bedroom and locking the door was my ritual, and that's when the excitement started."*

Acting Out

After the ritual happens, sexual acting out usually follows. This is often with pornography but could involve any sexual behavior. Afterward, the person feels terrible and uncomfortable, often experiencing shame, depression, and regret.

Pain/Shame

After acting out, a person is left with emotional pain or shame. Teens might feel depressed, weighed down by guilt, and disappointed in themselves, leading to a drop in self-esteem. This creates a build-up of emotional pressure inside them.

Withdraw

As the pain or shame increases, a person will withdraw from others and turn inward. This might involve hiding their behavior or pretending everything is fine when, deep down, they feel awful. This emotional isolation is like trying to keep the lid on a pressure cooker. The pressure builds, leading to more obsession—and the cycle continues.

10. Describe the kinds of "pain" or distress described in the cycle:

____

____

____

11. Describe any form of pain or distress that may be part of your own cycle:

____

____

____

12. Describe what "withdrawal," disconnection or isolation means in the cycle:

13. Describe the ways you withdraw, disconnection or isolate:

14. Describe what it feels like when you become "preoccupied" with sexual thoughts or behavior:

15. Describe your personal "rituals" that lead to sexually acting out. If needed, discuss this with your counselor:

16. List the acting out behaviors you are trying to eliminate in your life:

17. Why do you think most people addicted to pornography become skilled at hiding it? What are the costs of being honest about it?

____

____

____

____

Great job! You have completed all the lessons in Squire - Workbook 1.

Make sure to mark off the task lists and talk to your counselor or coach about a rank advancement.

APPENDIX

SQUIRE

WORKBOOK 1

JOURNAL NOTES

SOBRIETY TRACKER

MONTH:

SUNDAY	MONDAY	TUESDAY	WEDNESDAY	THURSDAY	FRIDAY	SATURDAY

MONTH:

SUNDAY	MONDAY	TUESDAY	WEDNESDAY	THURSDAY	FRIDAY	SATURDAY

MONTH:

SUNDAY	MONDAY	TUESDAY	WEDNESDAY	THURSDAY	FRIDAY	SATURDAY

MONTH:

SUNDAY	MONDAY	TUESDAY	WEDNESDAY	THURSDAY	FRIDAY	SATURDAY

SOBRIETY TRACKER

MONTH:

SUNDAY	MONDAY	TUESDAY	WEDNESDAY	THURSDAY	FRIDAY	SATURDAY

MONTH:

SUNDAY	MONDAY	TUESDAY	WEDNESDAY	THURSDAY	FRIDAY	SATURDAY

MONTH:

SUNDAY	MONDAY	TUESDAY	WEDNESDAY	THURSDAY	FRIDAY	SATURDAY

MONTH:

SUNDAY	MONDAY	TUESDAY	WEDNESDAY	THURSDAY	FRIDAY	SATURDAY

GOAL CHART

DATE:

GOALS	SUN	MON	TUES	WED	THURS	FRI	SAT

DATE:

GOALS	SUN	MON	TUES	WED	THURS	FRI	SAT

DATE:

GOALS	SUN	MON	TUES	WED	THURS	FRI	SAT

GOAL CHART

DATE:

GOALS	SUN	MON	TUES	WED	THURS	FRI	SAT

DATE:

GOALS	SUN	MON	TUES	WED	THURS	FRI	SAT

DATE:

GOALS	SUN	MON	TUES	WED	THURS	FRI	SAT

Congratulations for completing Workbook 1!

You have achieved Squire rank and have earned your first certificate. The next step on your journey will be found in Workbook 2 where you'll be promoted to Archer.

THE JOURNEY AHEAD

You're now equipped with tools and weapons to use in your fight against pornography and sexual compulsions or addictions. Keep referring to this Armory to help you throughout your recovery.

Your Valor group will be filled with new experiences and information for you to be successful. Work with your group, counselor or coach, and mentors through the Valor workbooks:

- **Workbook 1: Squire**
- **Workbook 2: Archer**
- **Workbook 3: Sergeant**
- **Workbook 4: Captain**
- **Workbook 5: Knight**

Guidebooks:

- **The Armory**
- **Mentor's Guide**
- **Parent's Guide**

Certificate of Completion

SQUIRE

Is Awarded To

____

This individual has completed all of the tasks for the rank of
Squire in the Valor™ Program.

____

Date

____

Therapist

REFERENCES

The Valor series materials were developed and influenced through clinical observation, professional research, collegial collaboration, and personal experience having worked in social services with adolescents over 30 years. The following organizations and resources were helpful in the development of this program:

- **SASH**
  (Society for the Advancement of Sexual Health)

- **IITAP**
  (International Institute for Treatment Addiction Professionals)

- **LifeSTAR**
  (Pornography and Sex Addiction Programming)

- **AASAT**
  (American Association for Sex Addiction Therapy)

- **AACC**
  (American Association of Christian Counselors)

Bowlby, J. (1988). *A secure base: Parent-child attachment and Healthy Human Development.* Basic Books.

Carnes, P. (1989). *Contrary to love: Helping the sexual addict.* Hazelden.

Carnes, P., & Carnes, P. (2001). *Out of the shadows: Understanding sexual addiction.* Hazelden Information & Edu.

Carnes, P., Delmonico, D., & Griffin, E. (2001). *In the Shadows of the Net: Breaking Free of Compulsive Online Sexual Behavior.* Hazelden.

Carnes, P., & Schwartz, B. K. (2010). *Facing the shadow: Starting sexual and relationship recovery: A gentle path to beginning recovery from sex addiction.* Gentle Path Press.

Carnes, P., Delmonico, D., & Griffin, E. (2001). *In The shadows of the net: Breaking free of compulsive online sexual behavior.* Hazelden.

Clear, J. (2018). *Atomic habits: An easy yet proven way to build good habits and break bad ones: Tiny changes, remarkable results.* Avery, an imprint of Penguin Random House.

Cline, F., & Fay, J. (2020). *Parenting with Love & Logic: Teaching Children Responsibility.* NavPress.

Diamond, D., Blatt, S. J., & Lichtenberg, J. D. (2014). *Attachment and sexuality.* Routledge.

Flores, P. J. (2004). *Addiction as an attachment disorder.* Jason Aronson.

Fortify: A step toward recovery. (2013). O.W.L. Publishing.

Gray, D., & Olson, T. (2012). *LifeSTAR Addiction Recovery Workbooks.* LifeSTAR Network.

Gray, D., & Olson, T. (2005). *Surviving Withdrawal - Laying the Groundwork for a Lasting Recovery.* LifeSTAR Network.

Home. Fight the New Drug. (2024, May 6). https://fightthenewdrug.org/

Kastleman, M. B. (2001). *The drug of the New Millennium: The Science of how internet pornography radically alters the human brain and body.* Granite Pub.

Katehakis, A., & Schore, A. N. (2016). *Sex addiction as affect dysregulation: A neurobiologically informed holistic treatment.* W.W. Norton & Company.

Laaser, M. R., & Laaser, M. R. (2004). *Healing the wounds of sexual addiction.* Zondervan.

Laaser, M. (1999). *Talking to your Kids about Sex.* Random House Publishing.

Mulligan, C. (2013). *How to recover from cyber pornography addiction: The teen cyber pornography.* Lulu Com.

Pollack, W. S. (1999). *Real boys: Rescuing our sons from the myths of boyhood.* H. Holt.

Schultz, E. (2023). *Healing the Invisible Scars: Nurturing the Journey to Emotional Wholeness.*

Wasserman, B. (1998). *Feeling good again: A workbook for children who have been sexually abused.* Safer Society Press.

Weiss, R., & Sack, D. (2015). *Sex addiction 101: A basic guide to healing from sex, Porn, and Love addiction.* Health Communications, Inc.

Weiss, R., & Schneider, J. P. (2014). *Closer together, further apart: The effect of Technology and the internet on parenting, work, and relationships.* Gentle Path Press.

Weiss, R., & Schneider, J. P. (2015). *Always turned on: Facing sex addiction in the Digital age.* Gentle Path Press.

Wilson, G. (2017). *Your brain on porn - internet pornography and the emerging science of addiction.* Commonwealth Publishing.

Wright, L. B., & Loiselle, M. B. (1997). *Back on track: Boys dealing with sexual abuse.* Safer Society Press.